SHOPS
A
is for
Apocalyptic
when things start going bad outside but
you and your family are safe because
you are prepped for any situation.

Ready Family
B
is for
Bugout Bag
A bugout bag is a special bag that you can grab in a hurry that has items you could live on for a few days

Wombat
READY
is for
Code Word
A special word, that when you hear it, it means time to go!

D
is for
Do It Yourself
it's important to learn how to do things yourself like build a shelter, fix a car, cook and grow your own food

E
is for
Emergency
In case of an emergency
make sure you know who
you need to contact

F
is for
First Aid
Sometimes people get hurt
and it's good to know how to
help them

READY
G is for
Gas Mask
They might look scary but they are just masks to keep you safe from bad smells

H
is for
Hunting
When the supermarkets run out of food, you will have to know how get your own meat.

I
HIDEOUT
is for
Isolation
Sometimes the best option is to leave and be with just your family and prepper tribe

J
is for Jeep
for when you have to go
off road to get to your
bug out locations

K
is for
karate
Learning self defence is important so you know how to defend yourself.

L
R
is for
Look and Listen
Always be on the lookout
for danger and always
listen to your parents

M
is for
Medicine
It is important to always
have enough medicine
on hand for any situation

is for Needy
People wanting to take what you have worked hard for

READY
is for Odd
Some people might call
preppers odd or other names,
but they don't matter
because you know you will be
ready when needed.

is for
Planning
Planning is the most important part of prepping
P
MOST
ToDo!

Q
R
is for
Quarantine
when you have to stay at home
to stop the spread of a virus

R
is for
Rally Point
This is a place where you know if something goes wrong, to go to this spot and wait for your family.

is for Safe house
This is a place where you know you will be safe and have supplies incase you need to leave your home.
S
HIDEOUT

is for Tribe
Your family and friends are going to combine and look after each other during the bad times

is for
Unstable
When the 'Needy" people start taking what they want, society becomes unstable.
U
SHOPS

is for
Vegetable Garden
Growing your own food is
the safest way to make
sure you have food

is for Work
Working hard is important for survival, and the best way to work is as a team
READY
W

is for
X-ray Delta Bravo
If you are going to learn
how to use a radio, you will
need to learn the phonetic
alphabet

Y
is for you
We all have our part to play, so make sure you listen to your parents and do as they say

is for Zen
above all else
remember to keep
claim, everything
is going to be OK
Z

THE
Ready
Family
#THEREADYFAMILY